Fact Finders®

→HOW LONG DOES IT TAKE FOR TRASH TO DECOMPOSE?

BY EMILY HUDD

CONTENT CONSULTANT
Ramani Narayan, PhD, University Distinguished Professor, Chemical Engineering and Materials Science, Michigan State University

CAPSTONE PRESS
a capstone imprint

Fact Finders Books are published by Capstone Press,
1710 Roe Crest Drive, North Mankato, Minnesota 56003
www.mycapstone.com

Library of Congress Cataloging-in-Publication Data
Names: Hudd, Emily, author.
Title: How long does it take for trash to decompose? / by Emily Hudd.
Description: North Mankato, Minnesota : Capstone Press, 2020 | Series: How long does it take? | Audience: Grades 4 to 6. | Includes bibliographical references and index.
Identifiers: LCCN 2018061100 (print) | LCCN 2019002321 (ebook) | ISBN 9781543572971 (ebook) | ISBN 9781543572919 (hardcover) | ISBN 9781543575422 (pbk.)
Subjects: LCSH: Refuse and refuse disposal--Environmental aspects--Juvenile literature. | Fills (Earthwork)--Juvenile literature. | Decomposition (Chemistry)--Juvenile literature. | Environmental chemistry--Juvenile literature.
Classification: LCC TD792 (ebook) | LCC TD792 .H83 2020 (print) | DDC 628.4/456--dc23
LC record available at https://lccn.loc.gov/2018061100

All internet sites appearing in back matter were available and accurate when this book was sent to press.

Editorial Credits
Editor: Marie Pearson
Designer and production specialist: Dan Peluso

Photo Credits
iStockphoto: CasarsaGuru, 14, f-1977, 23, Michael Burrell, cover (top), MoMorad, 5; Science Source: Gregory Davies/Medinet Photographics, 20; Shutterstock Images: Baloncici, 15, Belish, 21, davooda, 25 (paper), 25 (glass), 25 (aluminum), 25 (plastic bag), 25 (Styrofoam), Evan Lorne, 12, Fabrizio Misson, 11, Felix Mizioznikov, 7, Keep Calm and Vector, 25 (wool clothing), Kev Gregory, 28, Koryenyeva Tetyana, 27, monticello, 17, Rattiya Thongdumhyu, 8, Unkas Photo, 18; Unsplash: John Cameron, cover (bottom)

Design Elements: Red Line Editorial

TABLE OF CONTENTS

THROWING IT AWAY

A chef at a restaurant sweeps his hand across the counter. Lemon peels, bits of chicken, and bread crumbs fall into his hand. He throws them in the garbage. A woman on the street carries a plastic bag from a store. She tosses a gum wrapper into a trash can as she walks by. A student throws an empty yogurt cup in a bin.

The journey of trash can begin anywhere. It usually ends at the landfill. Some trash **decomposes** at the landfill. However, not all trash ends there. Some trash is **littered** and ends up where it doesn't belong.

decompose—to break down into smaller pieces

litter—to toss trash in a place where it does not belong, allowing it to end up in water or on land

Depending on what the trash is and where it ends up, it can take between 1 week and an estimated 1 million years for it to decompose.

People throw many things into the trash.

CHAPTER ONE

TRASH AT THE LANDFILL

Things become trash when they go into a garbage can. The trash can be there for several days before someone takes it out. A garbage truck collects the trash. Most trucks collect trash every week. The trucks take trash to the landfill.

One type of trash is **organic** waste, which includes recyclable trash. Examples of organic trash include pizza crusts, orange peels, paper, and cardboard. Another type of trash includes plastic, metal containers, and glass items. Trash is sorted at a landfill. Things that can be reused are saved. The rest is dumped in the landfill.

organic—made of material that was once living

Landfills are giant waste storage areas.

In a landfill, trash is dumped in a large hole in the ground. Some decomposes while it sits there. Decomposition is the process of breaking something down and changing it into simpler forms.

Anaerobes are too small for the human eye to see.

Anaerobes break down organic waste. Anaerobes are **microorganisms**. They work best in areas without air. Organic waste decomposes into gases. Metals, glass, and plastic break up slowly into small pieces. Anaerobes do not make them decompose.

The landfill hole has a liner. The liner lets very little liquid through. Beneath the liner is a layer of clay. The clay helps **absorb** unsafe chemicals, keeping them from leaking into the soil.

microorganism— a living thing that is too small to be seen without a microscope

absorb—to take in water

A few inches of soil are put between trash layers. The soil helps control the smell. It also protects the air. The layers absorb the landfill gas. Some landfills have pipes connected to them. The pipes collect landfill gas. The gas is burned to become energy for nearby cities.

Landfills protect people and Earth. They are located in areas without many people or animals. They are the end of the cycle for trash that is thrown away. However, too much trash is thrown into landfills. About 70 percent of waste in a landfill could be recycled or **composted**.

compost—to recycle organic matter so it becomes fertile soil

CHAPTER TWO

ORGANIC WASTE

Organic waste is made of material that was once living. It decomposes fairly quickly. Microorganisms, water, and sunlight break down organic waste. First, water, wind, and other forces break the waste into smaller pieces. Once the pieces are small, microorganisms break them down. Microorganisms change the waste into gases and **minerals**. Eventually, the organic waste becomes part of the soil. This natural process creates nutrients for the soil and air.

mineral—a material found in nature that is not an animal or plant

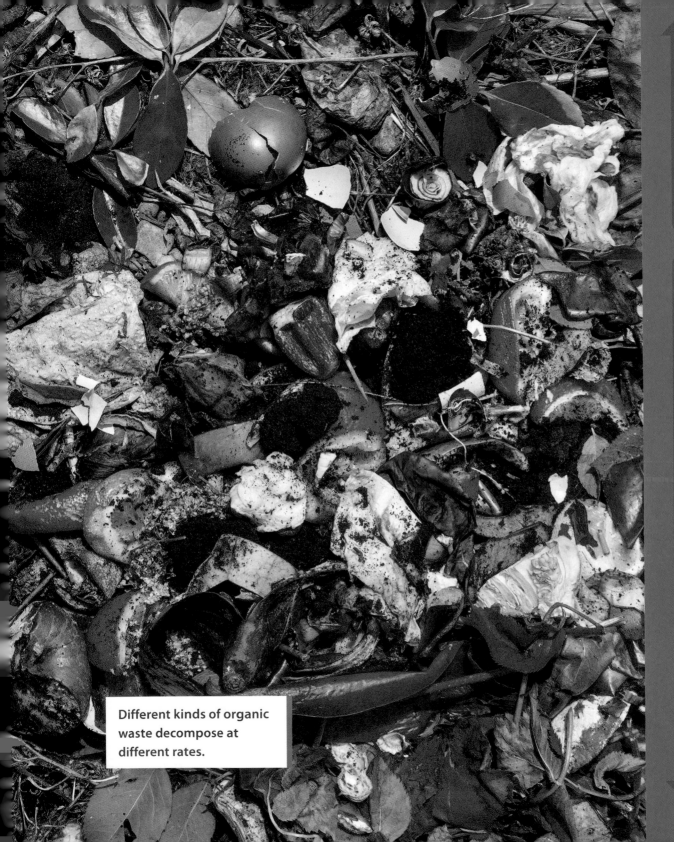

Different kinds of organic waste decompose at different rates.

Most organic waste in landfills takes months or years to break down. Newspaper takes about six weeks to decompose. Cardboard takes about two months.

Composting is a great way to reuse organic waste.

COMPOSTING

Composting is a natural process. It is a way to recycle organic matter like food and yard waste. Some people compost in their yards. It is usually done in a barrel or container. It gives off heat while the waste breaks down. Decomposition can take two months to two years. The compost can be used as **fertile** soil.

Pieces of wood can take one to three years. Wool clothing takes one to five years.

It is not good for organic waste to sit in landfills. It cannot release nutrients back to the soil. It should be composted. Composting is when aerobic microorganisms decompose organic waste. They break down waste, but they need air. Landfills are covered, so there is little or no air. In composting, the waste turns into nutrients for the soil. It helps plants grow.

fertile—having lots of nutrients to help plants grow better

Paper is often tied in bales to be recycled.

Some organic waste can be recycled. It can be reused. It may go through many uses before ending up in a landfill. Paper and cardboard are the

FACT Three times more paper is recycled than is sent to landfills.

most commonly recycled materials. Shoe boxes, cereal boxes, and paper from notebooks can all be recycled. They can also be composted.

The process starts when items are taken to recycling facilities. They are sorted by paper type and weight. Then they go to the paper mill. They are mixed with water. The water breaks up the paper into slurry. Slurry is a mix of paper pieces and water. Next, the mix is spread onto cloth or wire. As it dries, more layers are put on. It is dried in rolls. The rolls weigh as much as 2 tons (1.8 metric tons). Finally, it is ready to be turned into a new product.

Rolls of recycled paper can be cut and used for new products.

CHAPTER THREE

PLASTIC, GLASS, AND METALS

Plastic, glass, and metals take years to degrade. Degrading is a process where trash breaks into smaller and smaller pieces. It never completely goes away.

Glass is used today for bottles, mirrors, and more. Plastic is shaped into food containers and water bottles. Diapers have plastic in them too. Electronic devices like phones are made of plastic, glass, and metal parts. Soda cans are metal. All these materials last many years.

Plastic, glass, and metal trash
do not decompose. It takes a
long time for them to break up.

Plastic is made from small organic molecules
bonded together. It is water resistant and strong.
The bonds are difficult to break down. Plastic
doesn't typically break down into small, useful
parts. It just breaks up into smaller pieces of plastic.

The type of plastic determines how quickly it breaks up. The process can happen in days or many hundreds of years. Styrofoam is a foamed plastic made of tiny beads. It takes more than 50 years for Styrofoam to break up. A plastic bag may take 450 years to break up. In the ocean, plastic may take 80 to 200 years to break up. But scientists cannot observe such long processes. They do not know exactly how long these processes actually take.

Plastic bags harm wildlife and the environment.

RECYCLING PLASTIC

Plastic goes to a recycling facility to make it ready for reuse. In one method, workers sort it into similar types. Machines shred the plastic into tiny bits. Paper labels and other things are washed off the plastic. Another machine melts the plastic. The plastic is formed into small pellets. It's easy to make pellets into new shapes.

Plastic has to be exposed to sunlight to break up. Sunlight weakens the bonds slowly over time. First, the thin outer layer weakens. Water and air can then reach the surface of the plastic. The water and air help break the bonds, layer by layer. Finally, the plastic degrades into smaller and smaller pieces. Chemicals are released when the bonds break. They can **pollute** water or soil where the plastic is degrading.

FACT About 2 million plastic bags are used around the world every minute.

pollute—to make water, air, or something else dirty and potentially harmful to living things nearby

Glass can be made in different ways. One common glass is made by mixing lime, **silica**, and **sodium carbonate** in very high temperatures. Glass can be human-made or found in nature. It is extremely strong. It resists heat, water, and bacteria. It takes the longest of all materials to break up. Glass that is more than 1,500 years old has been found in Israel. Scientists think it could take more than 1 million years for glass bottles to break up.

A glass jar from hundreds of years ago can appear hardly changed.

silica—a part of sand

sodium carbonate—a chemical that can be used to make glass

When glass breaks up, the outer layer absorbs some water and flakes off. However, modern glass is made very carefully. The outer layer may only slightly flake.

The best option for glass is to recycle it. It can be crushed into small pieces. It is then melted and shaped into new products.

Glass is crushed during the recycling process so it melts easily.

RECYCLING METALS

Metal is recycled in a similar way to other materials. It is shredded, melted, and reused. Small cans aren't the only recycled metals. Metal from cars and other machines can be recycled too.

There are many different kinds of natural metals. To be useful, they need to be separated from the rocks they're found in. Some metals are then mixed together. This creates strong, man-made metals. Some metals break up into smaller pieces but never go away. Others break down from corrosion. Corrosion is when **oxygen** combines with metal surfaces and sometimes weakens them. Warm air and water can speed up corrosion. However, some metals have paint or coatings that protect them from corrosion.

oxygen—a gas that is used for many things on Earth, including breathing and breaking things down

Rusting is a form of corrosion.

Metal cans are a common piece of trash. Many food cans are made of thin steel. They can take 50 years to break up. Aluminum is a light metal. Many soda cans are made of it. It takes 200 to 500 years to break up.

 FACT Americans use 65 billion aluminum soda cans every year.

Electronic devices like computers often have metals. Smartphones are made of a combination of metal, glass, and plastic. This takes a long time to break up. When thrown away, electronics can also be dangerous.

Often, electronics have **toxic** materials. They have chemicals that are dangerous to living things. These toxins may leach, meaning seep out of, the devices. They can then seep into the ground. Some landfills have systems to collect and get rid of **leachate**. But lots of electronic waste is not thrown away properly. Or there might be a tear in the landfill lining. Leachate can harm animals, plants, and people nearby.

toxic—poisonous or potentially harmful
leachate—a mixture of toxins that seeps out of electronics and into the soil

ESTIMATED TIME TO DECOMPOSE OR BREAK UP

PAPER

6 weeks to decompose

WOOL CLOTHING

5 years to decompose

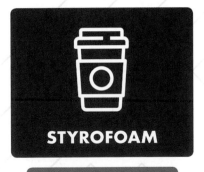

STYROFOAM

50+ years to break up

ALUMINUM

200–500 years to break up

PLASTIC BAG

450 years to break up

GLASS

1 million years to break up

CHAPTER FOUR

HOW TRASH AFFECTS EARTH

People sometimes throw fast food trash out of car windows and onto the street. Styrofoam containers and plastic bags blow away with the wind. One piece of trash may not seem like it matters. But litter adds up around the world.

Every year, Americans make 262 million tons (238 million metric tons) of waste. A little more than half ends up in landfills.

FACT
Cigarettes are the most common litter in the ocean. Plastic bottles and toys are also very common.

Litter blows around and can eventually end up in a body of water.

Trash that is not thrown away becomes litter. Litter pollutes Earth. Pollution is when human activity makes land, water, or air dirty and unsafe. Pollution harms all plants and animals.

When trash is not thrown away correctly, it often ends up in the ocean. Rain and rivers carry litter from land to bodies of water.

Plastic litter is a major problem in oceans. It breaks into tiny pieces of plastic, but it doesn't go away. Some animals eat it by accident.

Trash with holes can get caught around an animal's neck.

WORLD'S LARGEST TRASH COLLECTION

A collection of plastic trash is floating in the ocean between California and Hawaii. It is called the Great Pacific Garbage Patch. It is made of more than 1.8 trillion pieces of trash. Most of the trash is tiny pieces of plastic. The patch weighs more than 87,000 tons (79,000 metric tons). It's three times the size of France!

Fish, who need clean water, are surrounded by toxic water. Scientists estimate that at least 5.25 trillion pieces of plastic trash are in the ocean.

Trash needs to be thrown away or recycled correctly. It can take hundreds to millions of years to break up. In that time, it can pollute environments and harm living things.

FACT

About 80 percent of plastic in the ocean was first thrown away or littered on land.

GLOSSARY

absorb (ub-ZORB)—to take in water

compost (KAHM-pohst)—to recycle organic matter so it becomes fertile soil

decompose (dee-kum-POZE)—to break down into smaller pieces

fertile (FER-tuhl)—having lots of nutrients to help plants grow better

leachate (LEE-chate)—a mixture of toxins that seeps out of electronics and into the soil

litter (LIT-ur)—to toss trash in a place where it does not belong, allowing it to end up in water or on land

microorganism (mye-kroh-OR-guh-niz-um)—a living thing that is too small to be seen without a microscope

mineral (MIN-ur-uhl)—a material found in nature that is not an animal or plant

organic (or-GAN-ik)—made of material that was once living

oxygen (AHK-si-juhn)—a gas that is used for many things on Earth, including breathing and breaking things down

pollute (puh-LOOT)—to make water, air, or something else dirty and potentially harmful to living things nearby

silica (SIL-i-kah)—a part of sand

sodium carbonate (SOH-dee-um KAHR-buhn-ate)—a chemical that can be used to make glass

toxic (TAHK-sik)—poisonous or potentially harmful

ADDITIONAL RESOURCES

FURTHER READING

Chambers, Catherine. *How Effective Is Recycling?* Earth Debates. Chicago: Heinemann-Raintree, 2015.

Flynn, Riley. *Garbage Goes Out! What Happens After That?* The Story of Sanitation. North Mankato, Minn.: Capstone Press, 2019.

Rake, Jody Sullivan. *Endangered Oceans: Investigating Oceans in Crisis*. Endangered Earth. North Mankato, Minn.: Capstone Press, 2015.

CRITICAL THINKING QUESTIONS

1. Trash that is thrown away ends up at a landfill. Landfills can be helpful and harmful. What is one reason landfills are not the best place to put trash? What is one reason landfills are good for people and Earth?

2. Trash decomposes differently depending on what it is and where it lands. Choose one type of trash and describe how it decomposes. Use evidence from the text to support your answer.

3. Trash that is not thrown away becomes litter. Litter can cause pollution that harms Earth. Can you think of one way to help limit the amount of litter in the world?

INTERNET SITES

Environmental Protection Agency Kids: Recycle City
https://www3.epa.gov/recyclecity/

NASA Climate Kids: Meet the Greenhouse Gases!
https://climatekids.nasa.gov/greenhouse-cards/

National Geographic Kids: Plastic Pollution
https://kids.nationalgeographic.com/explore/nature/kids-vs-plastic/pollution/

INDEX

ABOUT THE AUTHOR

Emily Hudd is a full-time children's author who loves writing nonfiction on a variety of topics. She lives in Minnesota with her husband.